ADAM

THE MISSING LINK

LEON BIBI

DNA EVIDENCE OF MAN'S
ALIEN ORIGINS

LEON BIBI
Pegasus Publishing

Printed in the United States of America
First Printing 2021
First Edition 2021

10 9 8 7 6 5 4 3 2 1

DEDICATION

This book is dedicated to you-the independent thinker, the cerebral critic, the courageous theologian, the ambitious conspiracist, or even the puzzled anthropologist. It's easy to believe what billions of people espouse. After all, how could billions of people be wrong? How could a book, the most influential book in humankind, be wrong? How could the basic tenets of what we have learned regarding human beings' evolution be inaccurate?

This book is dedicated to you-the unfinished, imperfect, constantly learning human. Not afraid to look fiercely into the mirror. Not afraid to question the "undisputed". Not afraid to challenge the reigning champions of faith.

This book is written by someone whose interest lies in truth - not politics, or power. Not bound by any institution, governing body, or religion. Not shackled by vested interest. Not restricted by dogma.

This book is my last in the Adam Series™ and I am dedicated to enlighten you.

Lastly, in memory of Neil Peart, drummer of the rock band Rush. His rhythms, percussion and technical accuracy moved me and inspired me to play the drums. He is widely considered to be the greatest rock drummer of all time, and the band and its music gave me greater joy than I can even express.

R.I.P to the greatest of all.

"No his mind is not for rent,

to any God or government,

always hopeful yet discontent,

he knows changes aren't permanent,

but change is…"

– Neil Peart, Rush

TABLE OF CONTENTS

FOREWORD

"Without an understanding of who we are, and from where we came, I do not think we can truly advance"

- Louis B. Leakey, Archaeologist

"An honest man, armed with all the knowledge available to us now, could only state that in some sense, the origin of life appears at the moment to be almost a miracle, so many are the conditions which would have had to have been satisfied to get it going "

- Francis Crick Co-Discoverer of DNA

Being an avid history buff, I've always enjoyed reading and watching documentaries about everything from 9/11 to the Neanderthals. My father was a World War II veteran having served in Europe in the U.S. Army's unit - "Boys of Company C" - as an amphibious engineer. He was primarily responsible to rebuild bridges that had been blown up by the Nazis, in order to circumvent the Allies' progress. He was very successful, having earned multiple Medals of Honor for bravery during combat.

Fortunately, while he may have killed many Nazis during his 3-year service in Europe , he was never shot himself. Having lived happily to the age of 94, I can clearly remember all of his stories. Stories of fun and stories of danger.

Regarding prehistory, and specifically the Sumerian Tablets, I never understood the following:

- Why did the British excavate in Mosul, Iraq?
- Why did the French excavate in Khorsabad, Iraq?
- Why did the Russians excavate in Babylon, (Bagdad) Iraq?
- Why during the US invasion of Iraq did the US Army storm the Baghdad Museum?

In all of these cases the British, French, Russians, and the Americans kept everything to themselves and never shared what they have found. 15,000 pieces of antiquity were taken from the Baghdad Museum which were at least 6,000 years old. Why are these Sumerian Tablets so coveted? What esoteric information do they contain? Could it be that the British, French, Russians and Americans know exactly what they contain? I believe the answer to this is YES.

What's so important about these tablets? Why are they exhibited in the following museums - The Iraqi museum in Baghdad, the British museum, Berlin Museum, the Louvre, the Istanbul archaeology Museum, the Brussels Cinquantenaire Museum, and L'Ermitage de Saint-Petersbourg Museum in Russia?

It is my firm belief that the information specifically detailed in the Sumerian Tablets contains the answers to the questions at the forefront of medicine and evolution. The answers that have been hidden from 99% of all the humans of the world for the past 4000 years. Answers that would rock the foundation of science and religion. They answer-

- Who are we?
- How were we made?
- Who or What is God?
- How are math and physics related to the complex structure of the universe?
- Are extraterrestrials real?

Only 3% of our genes are coded and active, we can read them and decode them. This leaves 97%, or "Junk DNA" that are non coded, and cannot be converted to protein. What's very interesting to scientists today is that within the 97% junk DNA lies "telomerase". Telomerase is defined in Wikipedia as:

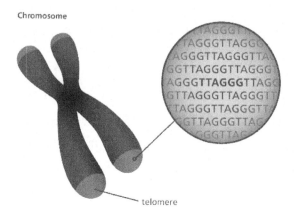

Chromosome

telomere

Telomerase, *also called terminal transferase, is a ribonucleoprotein that adds a species-dependent telomere repeat sequence to the 3' end of telomeres. A telomere is a region of repetitive sequences at each end of eukaryotic chromosomes in most eukaryotes.*

In 2018, **Science Daily**, reported the following -

*"Research from the laboratory of Professor Julian Chen in the School of Molecular Sciences at Arizona State University recently uncovered a crucial step in the telomerase enzyme catalytic cycle. This catalytic cycle determines the ability of the human telomerase enzyme to synthesize DNA "repeats" (specific DNA segments of six nucleotides) onto chromosome ends, **and so afford immortality in cells.** Understanding the underlying mechanism of telomerase action offers new avenues toward effective **anti-aging therapeutics**..*

Why can't we tap in to junk DNA? Based on reading the Sumerian Tablets it could be assumed that our makers literally *turned off* the ability to tap into junk DNA and possible immortality. Just imagine how we humans could be changed forever if we were able to tap into junk DNA.

CHAPTER 1

GENE-SIS 223

"It is the rare scientist, indeed, that will even consider the evidence... The scientific Community, by and large, would rather it all just went away, would rather be able to preclude it from consideration, consign it to The Lunatic Fringe with sarcasm and ridicule. "

- Neil Freer, *God Games*

"While the scientific imperialists and the religious dogmatists have thought that they owned the discussion by proprietarily boxing the argument and defining the binary options, the Sumerian scholar, Zecharia Sitchin, has advanced a robust and coherent paradigm of our genesis and unique history that, if true, and I'm convinced that it is after working critically with it for 32 years , is profound, comprehensive, and fundamental enough to enable us to rewrite the entire history of our beginnings and the planet astronomically, evolutionarily, paleontologically, archaeologically, and literally redefine ourselves as Humans."

- Neil Freer, *Sapiens Rising*

To quote one of my favorite authors - Neil Freer - regarding the state of evolution theory - "*It is well to remind ourselves, as Wilson does, that this position of science concerning evolution is the 'legacy of the last century of scientific research*". *To be more precise, it is the legacy of late 19th century thinking in science and religion. Darwin's theory of evolution was published in 1859, about 140 years ago, and it has been disputed in general or in detail since then. The Lamarckian versus the Darwinian versus the Durkheim / Radcliffe-Brown controversies seem to be over specific mechanisms rather than overarching explanations. There has been no major counter theory to replace it so far...something is still lacking in the consensual theory of evolution as it applies to human nature. When the recently determined, puzzling sequence of development, which sees Homo Sapiens co-existent with Neanderthals and even proceeding them, is taken into consideration the clues are reinforced: the basic premise of natural selection is contradicted if the more evolved species precedes the less evolved.*" (Freer)

Shouldn't the correct order of species be, according to Darwin and established science, apes before any type of humans? The more primitive humans would evolove from the apes. Therefore Homo Habilus before Homo Erectus, and Homo Erectus before Homo Sapiens. Where do the

Anunnaki come in? Was it at the Cro-Magnon level or the Homo Erectus level?

Mitochondrial evidence suggests that our first woman ancestor came from east central Africa. Was this a "synthetic genesis" of a "synthesized species"?

Artist rendering of Homo Erectus

Is it a coincidence that ancient gold mines were also found in east central Africa with 100,000 year old human skeletal remains - 80 feet down in the mines? Was this the location of the Anunnaki laboratory in which humans were first created?

"Only recently genetic researchers have suggested that there is evidence of alien sequences in our genetic code "

- Freer, *Sapiens Rising*

"Behold, the Adam has become as one of us ... "

- Sumerian tablets

Caduceus Symbol of Medicine

I'd like you to take a look at today's Caduceus symbol of Medicine (see above). In the middle is a long staff. On each side a pair of wings, similar to an eagle's wings. Wrapped around the staff are two snakes. Take a long look at it. Could this not be a representation of DNA coming from the heavens?

The two snakes represent the two strands of chromosomes, while the wings represent coming from heaven or Heaven above.

The staff represents authority or the initiator of this symbol. To me, this makes perfect sense and represents the symbol of medicine to be DNA- having originated from heaven or our maker's hands.

Sumerian Tree of Life

Caduceus Symbol in Antiquity?

Caduceus Symbol in Ancient Greece

What's interesting is that in both the Sumerian Tablets and the Old Testament, DNA is referred to as the "Essence of Life". *Essence* is the intrinsic basis of something. How could the early scribes of the Sumerian Tablets and the Old Testament have known about DNA? It wasn't discovered until 1950. What's also interesting is that the "Tree of Knowing" is also discussed in both the Sumerian Tablets and the Old Testament. We know that this can't be an actual tree, so then does it symbolize something deeper?

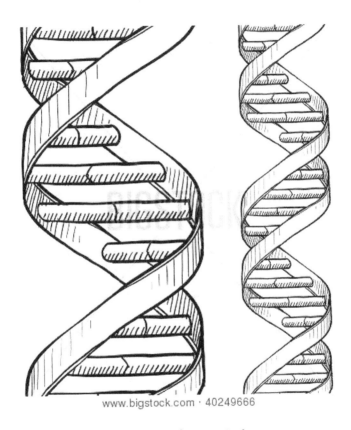

Diagram of DNA Coils

If we observe a diagram of DNA we can notice 2 spiral strands coiling around each other. These strands are pairs of chromosomes. Does the Tree of Knowing with its coiling branches refer specifically to chromosomes in DNA? Is it possible that the Gods knew that the essence of a human being lie in its DNA? That DNA was both the Essence of Life and the Tree of Knowledge.

There are 22 different body types that exist on the world - 22 different human forms - Asian, African, Indian, Aboriginal, Anglo-Saxon, South American, Nordic, Ottoman, Arabic and many others. Why 22? Have there been 22 different alterations in our genome over the past 250,000 years?

There are **223 genes** in the human genome that have no predecessors - not primate or any other species. They just *appeared* there like magic. Where did they come from?

What separates us physically from primates?

- Foreheads
- Hardly any brow ridge
- Rectangular eye sockets vs. Round
- Small nasal passages
- Small flat mouths
- Chin
- Less bone density and musculature
- Unique skin
- Sweat and glandular secretions
- Body hair
- Unique throats

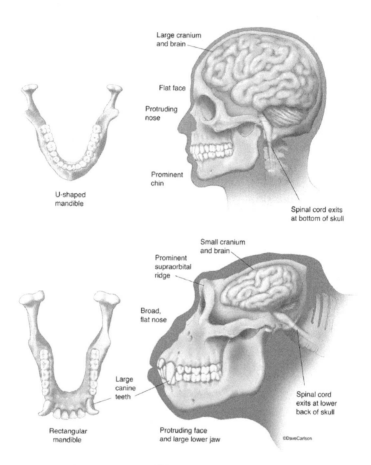

A comparison of Human versus Ape Skulls

What separates us biologically from primates?

- Larger brains - 1400 cc versus 950 cc
- Ability to speak and reason
- 4,000 genetic defects (Diabetes, auto-immune disorders, etc.)

"The ancient records could be interpreted to mean either a complete melding of the two codes or, alternatively, the impingement of selected Anunnaki genes on the Homo Erectus code to tweak up the more primitive code to at least a condition of intelligence and physical competence to handle the mining of gold " - Freer, *Sapiens Rising*

Could our genome be made up of Enki's (and Ninmah's or Ningishzidda's) genes? Could the original Adam and Eve be a result of these gods' genes mixed with the most intelligent primate species on Earth at the time - Homo Erectus- 200,000 years ago? Homo Erectus hadn't evolved significantly for the previous 1.5 million years, yet, all of a sudden, he mutated to the Homo Sapien. How can this be?

DNA is not just a blueprint or a code. It appears to be a liquid of varying, flexible viscosity.

The brain is not just a measure of intelligence. It is a quantum entanglement computer that can actually bend energy!

CHAPTER 2

MYTHINFORMATION

"It is remarkable that Darwinism is accepted as a satisfactory explanation for such a vast subject - evolution - with so little rigorous examination of how well it's basic theses work and Illuminating specific instances of biological adaptation or diversity."

- Microbiologist James Shapiro

"We exist on a lonely speck of sand which revolves around an average-sized star on the outskirts of an unexceptional galaxy, which is one of approximately 50 billion galaxies in the known universe."

- Joe Lewels - *The God Hypothesis*

"To suppose that Earth is the only populated world in infinite space, is as absurd as to believe that an entire field sown with millet, only one grain will grow"

- *Metrodorus of Chios* - 4th Century B.C.

"Innumerable suns exist; innumerable Earths revolve around these suns in a manner similar to the way the seven planets revolve around our sun. Living beings inhabit these worlds"

- Giordano Bruno - Italian philosopher burned at the Stake during the Inquisition in 1600

For all those who cracked the code in "Adam Decoded - Volume 2", I congratulate you.

The code signifies my core thesis - that human beings are not a direct result of straight Darwinist evolutionary mutation. Something intervened which jump-started our huge advances in mathematics, architecture, astronomy, commerce, and our political / social structure. The Sumerians were the first true human culture that originated from our Anunnaki makers. The Sumerians worshipped them- building extraordinary monuments, pyramids and architecture and then something quite extraordinary happened....

The Anunnaki left.

Image of Anunnaki

They were successful in their mission to extract vast amounts of gold from Earth and transported it to their home planet of Nibiru. Homo Sapiens were a by-product of this necessity, as the Anunnaki needed slave labor to dig the gold. It was an arduous process, even with the use of lasers, high-speed drills and huge circular saws. The Anunnaki needed a (semi) intelligent humanoid, with an increased brain capacity to reason and think on their own - a huge upgrade from the muscular brute (Cro-Magnon) that had already existed on Earth in 445,000 BC.

This enlarged brain capacity, which jumped from 950cc to 1350cc almost overnight, is responsible for today's 21st century advances. Advances in all areas of knowledge which culminated in an understanding of the basic workings of the cosmos. We were no longer just trying to survive. We were developing into a fourth density sentient being - not a small feat in less than 500,000 years!

The Sumerian civilization who lived during the Anunnaki reign produced hundreds of thousands of clay cuneiform tablets - 300,000 of which have been found to date.

Doubting Darwin

Our DNA code was cracked in the 1950's.

Essentially today there are two groups of thought regarding evolution. The Darwinists who believed that evolution has modified from simplicity to complexity through alterations. The Creationists who believe that a Supreme Being created humans through no alterations. However in the "*The Origin of Species* " Darwin never actually used the word " evolution" to describe the process underlying his theory, he called it "natural selection". But there are several problems related to Darwin's theory:

1. <u>The Cambrian Explosion</u> - A sudden, abrupt evolution teeming with life forms that did not evolve and/or mutate slowly.

2. <u>Phyla</u> - 26 phyla appeared during the Cambrian explosion, however no new phyla appeared thereafter.

"What the fossil record actually reveals is that every class, order, family, genus, or species simply appears, fully formed and ready to eat, survive and reproduce. And they all exhibit a certain range of physical variation that is sometimes wide and sometimes narrow" - Pye - Everything You Know is Wrong

3. <u>Australopithecus</u> - The Homo Erectus line could not have simply evolved from the Australopithecines based upon skull structure and brain power. Homo Erectus skulls demonstrate a sharp reduction in skull size with the jawline ostensibly rounding out the braincase. They underwent a 50% increase in brain power from 500cc to 750cc literally overnight.

4. <u>Neanderthals</u> - are **not related** to modern humans.

This is a modern fallacy. While their own brain and body size did increase, their skeletal structure remains completely unique and does not correlate to human body structure. They may be a developed bipedal primate, but they are not related to humans. In an analysis of Neanderthal DNA recently recovered, out of 378 genetic base pairs compared with humans, 28 mismatches were found.

"For now we can leave the Darwinists scrambling to plausibly explain how 4.0 million years of supposed evolutionary progress could so clearly point to the development of a robustly built, massively muscled, rather dimwitted brute; Then suddenly, at only 120,000 years ago, modern humans appear - as if by magic!- To live alongside their cousins while looking almost nothing like them" - Pye - **Everything You Know is Wrong**

We couldn't have developed from the Neanderthals because the fossil records show that we were living with them, side-by-side, at the same time. Author Gregg Braden cites the following –

*"In a report published in the prestigious journal **Nature**, researchers at the University of Glasgow's Human Identification Centre described their investigation comparing the genetic material from our possible ancestors to that of modern humans. Along with co-workers in Russia and Sweden in 1987 the scientists tested ancient DNA from the body of an unusually well preserved Neanderthal infant, discovered in a limestone cave of the northern Caucasus....While scientists are still reeling from the implications of the report, the study found that the possibility of a genetic link between Neanderthals and modern humans was remote. The results suggest that 'modern man was not, in fact, descended from Neanderthals'."* - **Nature,** volume 404, 3/30/2000, pg 490.

5. Cro-Magnon - **<u>are related</u>** to modern humans. While Neanderthals all died out 30,000 years ago, Cro-Magnons which initially began to appear around 120,000 years ago and lived until 35,000 years ago. Unlike Neanderthals, their skull shape looks very similar to ours. Their high foreheads which held a 1400cc brain capacity matches the current shape of ours. They also displayed cave art 20,000 years ago which show remarkable intelligence

Mem = Water = Oxygen

Shem = Fire = Hydrogen (or even propulsion as "shem" is "rocket" in Sumerian)

It's also interesting to note that the Hebrew letter Aleph א who's sound is silent , has the shape of DNA.

All life is formed as combinations of only four chemical compounds - Adenine (A), Thymine (T), Guanine (G), and Cytosine (C) - also called DNA "bases". The bases arrange themselves into precise pairs known as "base pairs". The different combinations of base pairs are known as "genes". Groups of genes that form 23 pairs are called "chromosomes". While the DNA molecule excels at stocking and duplicating information it is still incapable of building itself on its own.

Interestingly if we compared the name of man in Hebrew (YHVG) and the name of God in Hebrew (YHVH), and equated each letter to its chemical equivalent, the only difference is that God's chemical equivalent is nitrogen and man's chemical equivalent is carbon. Knowing that carbon is the predominant element in the human body - 18% by mass, **can it be that only this component separates us from the elements of God? Carbon?**

In the several documents leaked through Freedom of Information Act, extraterrestrials specifically the "greys" have referred to humans as "**containers**". This definition has baffled scientists with above-top-secret clearance for the past 70 years. The closest analysis that I can give would be that we are containers of souls, since our soul is what appears to separate us from these extraterrestrials. Amazingly, Braden uses the same terminology when he discusses DNA. He says the following -

*"Through the primal act of creating human life, God shared a part of himself as he 'breathed his breath' into our species. In doing so, we assumed the role of 'vessels', uniquely endowed with the divine spirit. To this day, our role continues, as the ancient secret to creating such a **container** is preserved and passed on through the miracle of each new human life.*

Perhaps the answer to the mystery of what makes us different remains hidden within the tiny molecule that holds life's code itself: our DNA." (page 162).

This is incredible. Could the grey extraterrestrials be talking about DNA separating us from themselves preserved in containers? Our bodies could be considered as containers of DNA, couldn't they?

"Elaborating upon the description of our bodies as structures housing God's Essence, the Kabbalah invites us even deeper into the mystery, describing how the containers of God's light (the vessels) shattered and fell into the lower spiritual realms of Earth. Here in the Earthly realms where Darkness and Light coexist, the vessels reformed and were able to communicate their light to the world of humans." (page 163).

223

We know today and have identified **223 genes** that have no predecessor. Isn't it interesting that he also points out that The 22 letters of the Hebrew alphabet interconnect to create our world. *"If we use all of the combinations of letters and arrange them graphically as a circle there are 231 lines that connect the possibilities.*

The Sepher Yetzirah identifies these lines as the 231 'Gates'" (page 57). Can these Gates be related to Heaven's Gate?

Can Heaven's Gate be related to a Stargate?

Another amazing quote from Braden- how the four corners of the Earth may represent a pyramid, and that this pyramid form may be an element of DNA - *"The oral traditions of the Midrash and early Kabbalah, for example, describe how the Creator asked his angels to 'go and fetch me dust from the **four corners** of the earth and I will create man therewith'"* (page 68). The G, A, C and D proteins in DNA may also be a representation of the "four corners", couldn't they?

Author Bruce Fenton of *Hybrid Humans,* posts the following on their website, www.earthancients.com, which sheds light onto our current knowledge that aliens created man. Below is an excerpt from their website-

On the 9th of April, 1983, noted investigative reporter, Linda Moulton Howe, met with Sgt. Richard Doty of the Air Force Office of Special Investigations. The appointment had been arranged (with) the understanding that this would initiate collaboration between the US Air Force and Moulton Howe in the creation of a documentary film. The film production was supposed to share official records of UFOs and extraterrestrial beings with the public. The first files to be shared were supposed to provide details on a purported UFO landing at Ellsworth Air Force Base.

In a supposedly private room at Kirtland Air Force Base (it was later confirmed the room was secretly filmed) Doty evaded questions about the Ellsworth landing and instead handed Moulton Howe a document that he said his superiors wanted her to see. The first line of the papers offered the bold statement **'Briefing Paper for the President of the United States on the subject of Unidentified Ariel Vehicles (UAVs)'.** This was certainly not what this seasoned journalist had been expecting to happen, and when Doty added that she could not take any notes, she was left wondering what on earth this strange situation was all about.

Natural curiosity led to an examination of the document, in which several secret projects were highlighted and summarised as well as locations for various crashed saucer craft recovered by the US military. The list of secretive projects included Aquarius, Snowbird, Garnet, Moondust, and Pounce. The project that really stood out for Moulton Howe was Garnet, firstly because it shared its name with her birthstone, secondly because it was not about aerial craft but instead claimed to have "answered all questions and mysteries about the evolution of *Homo sapiens* on this planet".

Associated with the investigation of Project Garnet were two further incredible revelations, one was that "extraterrestrials had manipulated DNA in an already evolving primate species to create *Homo sapiens*" and the second that "2000 years ago the extraterrestrials had created a being to put on this planet to teach *Homo sapiens* about love and non-violence".

As we approach the 35th anniversary of this extraordinary meeting we would like to reveal that our research team has now corroborated the central findings claimed by Project Garnet. We can confirm that there is physical and biological evidence of the engineering of *Homo sapiens* by an alien presence on earth almost 800,000 years ago. We can tell you where they came from, what type of craft they arrived in, which genes they modified and where they set up their laboratory. In fact, we can even identify debris from their wrecked mothership.

We feel that 35 years of secrecy on the matter of human origins needs to be ended and that all humans have a right, indeed a need, to know the truth of our shared origins. Our species is a hybrid of early *Homo* and Star People that arrived here from a wormhole linking our planet and the Pleiades star cloud. This is not a channelled message or an interpretation of any ancient carvings, there is no reliance on whispers from black project agents – with help from my husband, <u>Bruce R. Fenton</u>, I have identified the physical material from a craft and genetic data in the human genome that scientists in project Garnet uncovered in their investigation. We did this as grassroots researchers free from collusion or contamination.

We do not offer disclosure of any government UFO projects, that is beyond our abilities at this time, but from April 15th we will be able to provide you with solid Ancient Alien Ancestors disclosure. The material we have gathered together rewrites everything humanity thought they knew about human origins. Join us on the journey of a lifetime, it is time to meet the Pleiadian progenitors who birthed *Homo sapiens* 780,000 years ago in Australia

She then read a paragraph that said the Extraterrestrials had manipulated DNA in an already evolving primate species to create Homo Sapiens. That sentence really astonished her as she read it over and over again to (soak) in the words. It also caused her to think of other questions such as: is this linked to genetic harvests in animal mutilations? Are they using animals from earth to create other androids? What service do humans provide them?

ADAM / THE MISSING LINK

Another paragraph went on to state that 2000 years ago the Extraterrestrials had created a being to put on this planet to teach Homo Sapiens about love and non-violence. When Howe read this she said out loud "We are talking about Jesus Christ" Howe say that Doty did not say a word, but that he turned red". www.earthancients.com.

CHAPTER 4

HOMO ERECTUS ANUNNAKIS

" I will form blood and let Bones come to be. Then I will make the human being, his name shall be man. Yes, I will make the human!"

- Marduk - The Enuma Elish

"Findings in the fossil record contradict the Darwinian view that species arise gradually over long periods of time. In fact, there is no evidence for the gradual appearance of one species out of another. There is no evidence of intermediate species, linking one form to another, as with Homo Sapiens"

- Joe Lewels - The God Hypothesis

Are we really Homo Erectus *Nefilimus*? A genetically engineered species going through a rapid metamorphosis? If it's true that Nibiru (Planet X) is indeed headed into our solar system and is the actual home of the Anunnaki, then couldn't all the archaelogical evidence of 8ft-12ft tall skeletons found worldwide corroborate this thesis?

If Sitchin is correct and the Anunnaki did in fact create Home Sapiens, couldn't (and shouldn't) his work be as important as Darwin's *Origin of Species?*

Shouldn't all the ancient texts and Sumerian tablets found and are demonstrated in major museums throughout the world, support this thesis?

"Enki, their Chief scientist and Ninhursag their chief medical officer, after getting no satisfactory results splicing animal and Homo Erectus genes, merged their Anunnaki genes with that of Homo Erectus and produced us ." - Freer

DNA is tiny, but miraculous. Lloyd Pye explains -

"The coils of DNA that make up the chromosomes in the nuclei of living cells are microscopically small marvels of biological engineering. It is estimated that if all the DNA in one cell nucleus was stretched out like a string, it would reach from 3 ft. at the low end to 9 ft. at the high end; yet it is so tightly wound inside the nucleus it is like a wad of rubber bands- around anywhere from 1/100,000 to 1/2,000000 the size of the head of a pin!" - Pye - Everything You Know is Wrong

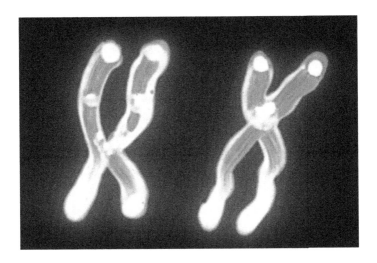

Actual DNA Coils

In order to create the Adam, The Annunaki would have to cross fertilize two species - themselves and the Cro-Magnon. However, the genes in at least one gamete (definition: *a mature haploid male or female germ cell which is able to unite with another of the opposite sex in sexual reproduction to form a zygote*) have to be altered.

Pye now explains what is needed:

"Of our two available choices for manipulation, female ovum (eggs) are much larger and easier to work with than sperm cells. In fact, sperm cells are so tiny (thousands could fit inside a single egg), they can be considered impossible to alter. So female eggs are what must be changed.

Now, should we modify the gorilla eggs to make them more closely aligned with the genes in human sperm, or vice versa? Since gorillas have 24 chromosomes per sex cell and humans 23, one or the other figure must be chosen; Either reduce the gorillas down to 23, or increase humans up to 24. However, an entire chromosome cannot be taken from or added to any creature without altering critical genes, so the only alternative is to **combine two chromosomes into one** (author's underline) *((remember this!)) by splicing"* - Pye - Everything You Know is Wrong

"I will produce a lowly primitive,

'Man' shall be his name.

I will create a primitive worker;

He will be charged with the service of the gods,

That they might have their ease."

"Shaggy with hair is his whole body :

He is endowed with head-hair like a woman.

He knows neither people nor land:

Garbed he is like one of from green fields;

With gazelles he feeds on grass ;

With wild beasts he jostles at the watering place." - *Sumerian tablets 2500BC*

Isn't this interesting? First, you will notice that the Sumerians wrote in poetic form. You will notice that they will speak almost in a backwards form - "*Garbed he is*", "*With gazelles he feeds*", etc...almost Shakespearean - demonstrating a great intellect. Second, doesn't the second paragraph sound like the description of a Cro-Magnon? Can this possibly be a complete coincidence written 4500 years ago? Is that even remotely possible?

Or can it be that the gods who created us, were describing the first Proto-human creation?

The name for this new being was called "the Adam" because he was created out of the "Adama" or the Earth's soil. After the first being was created, further beings (plural) were called "Adamu".

CHAPTER 5

CHROMOSOME 2

"Sooner or later we have to come to grips with the unbelievable notion that every life form on Earth carries genetic code for his extraterrestrial cousin and that evolution is not what we think it is."

- Professor Sam Chang - The Human Genome Project

Chromosomes contain biological instructions that determine bone structure, brain size, metabolic processes, and other functions. Braden comments -

*"A closer look at the chromosomes that appear to be absent from our gene pool shows that human chromosome 2 is remarkably similar and actually 'corresponds' to chromosomes 12 and 13 of the chimpanzee, **as if they were to be combined** (fused) into a single larger piece of DNA "* - Braden - page 31

As humans have 46 chromosomes and gorillas/chimps have 48 chromosomes, was there actually a fusion event between the two? If so, are there any markers - like extra telomeres or extra cetromeres? The answer is YES - on chromosome 2.

Chromosome 2 demonstrates nearly identical DNA sequences as chimp chromosomes, as if they were "snipped together".

From the Institute for Creation Research, Dr. Jeffrey Tompkins from Clemson University states-

"In 2002, 614,000 bases of DNA surrounding the fusion site were fully sequenced, revealing that the alleged fusion sequence was in the middle of a gene originally classified as a pseudogene, because there was not yet any known function for it. The research also showed that the genes surrounding the fusion site in the 614,000-base window did not exist on chimpanzee chromosomes 2A or 2B - the supposed ape origins location. In genetics terminology, we call this discordant gene location a lack of synteny" - Jeffrey Tompkins, PhD.

Chromosome Counts-

Humans, Neanderthals and Denisovans - 46

Gorillas, Bonobos and Chimpanzees – 48

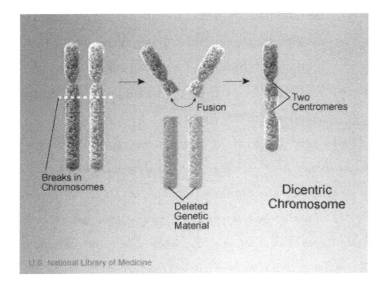

Photo of a fused chromosome above.

There are at least 3 DNA genes that I know of that sets us apart from chimps and apes.

- MIR-941 -a brain gene that gives us an edge over apes and chimps, which the study suggests is carried only by humans. This data was corroborated in **Science** from November 14, 2011.

- SRGAP2 - Humans have 23 copies of a gene known as SRGAP2 involved in brain development. Chimps and orangutanes have only one copy.
- FOXP2 - This is another gene that sets us apart from chimps and apes called FOXP2 which gives us the ability to speak- the language gene. This has been one of the hardest genes for scientists to crack..
- RPTN, SPAG17,CAN15, TTFI, PCD16 and many others add to this mystery.

"People have 23 pairs of chromosomes, for a total of 46 chromosomes. Most apes have 24 pairs of chromosomes, for a total of 48 chromosomes. One very popular piece of genetic evidence for the idea that humans and apes have a common ancestor is that human chromosome 2 looks like two chimpanzee chromosomes that have been stitched together. As the evolutionary story goes, the common ancestor between apes and humans had 24 pairs of chromosomes, and it initially passed them to those animals that began evolving into apes and humans. The apes kept that number of chromosomes, but after the human lineage split off from the chimpanzee lineage, something happened to fuse two of the chromosomes, leading to only 23 pairs of chromosomes in humans. - Dr. Francis Collins

The fusion that occurred as we evolved from the apes has left its DNA imprint here. It is very difficult to understand this observation without postulating a common ancestor.

Dr. Jeffrey P. Tomkins, a former director of the Clemson University Genomics Institute, recently published a paper in which he analyzed the genetic content of the site at which this fusion was supposed to have taken place. In the DNA of eukaryotes (all organisms whose cells have a nucleus), genes are composed of two regions: **exons** and **introns**. When the information in a gene is copied so the cell can use it to make a protein, both the introns and the exons are copied. Before the copy is used to make the protein, however, the introns are removed, as shown in this figure:

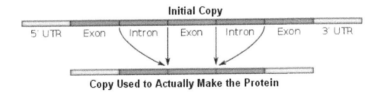

Genes are composed of exons interrupted by 'spacers' known as introns.

In other words, the exons are the parts of the gene that contain the information the cell needs, in order to make a specific protein. The introns are "spacers" that separate these chunks of information. Why is a gene constructed this way? Because each exon is a *module* of information, and the modules can be put together in many different ways. As a result, many different proteins can be made from a single gene. This process is called <u>alternative splicing</u>, and it vastly increases the amount of information that DNA can store. Indeed, there is a specific human gene that can be used to make *576 different proteins* thanks to the way its introns and exons are arranged. In the fruit fly, there is a specific gene that can be used to make *38,016 different proteins!* This is just one of the many features of DNA that shows it is the result of incredible design.

So here's where Dr. Tomkins's research gets interesting: He found that the place on chromosome 2 where the two chromosomes are supposed to have fused is *right in the intron of a gene!* The gene is charmingly named *DDX11L2*, and it is known to be used in several different cells, including those performing tasks related to the nervous system, muscle system, immune system, and reproductive system.

CHAPTER 6

COLD FUSION

"When DNA speaks, everybody listens"

- Neil Freer, *God Games*

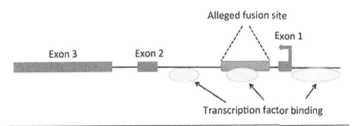

Transcription factor binding sites in DDX11L2.

Alleged fusion site in DDX11L2

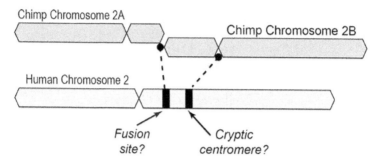

Alleged chimpanzee chromosomes 2A and 2B fused end-to-end to form a human

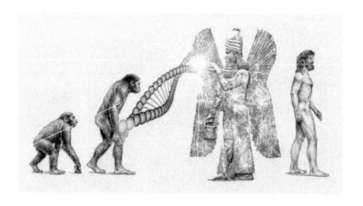

What makes us human? Some say that it is the development of language, though others argue that animals have language as well. Some say that it is our ability to use tools, though many animals are able to use rocks and other objects as primitive tools.

Now, researchers believe that they have found the definitive difference between humans and other primates, and they think that the difference all comes down to a single gene.

Researchers from the University of Edinburgh in Scotland attribute the split of humanity from apes to the gene **MIR-941**. They say that the gene played an integral role in human development and contributed to humans' ability to use tools and learn languages.

Most of the time, when one species diverges from another, that difference occurs because of gene mutations, duplications, or deletions. However, this gene is believed to have emerged, fully functional, from "junk DNA" in a breathtakingly short amount of evolutionary time.

Humans share 96 percent of their genes with other primates. Of the 4 percent that humans alone have, a significant portion of it has been widely labeled "junk DNA". Researchers have since learned that "junk DNA" is functional, even though it does not code. This is the first time that a gene that humans and other primates do not share has been shown to actually have a specific function within the body.

Researchers came to this conclusion after comparing the human genome to 11 other species of mammals, including gorillas, chimpanzees, mice, and rats. These comparisons were made so that the geneticists could find the difference between them.

In a study published in "*Nature Communications*", researchers say that the gene emerged sometime between six and one million years ago.

The gene is highly active in the regions of the brain that control language learning and decision making, indicating that it may play a significant role in the higher brain functions that make humans, well, human.

CHAPTER 7

THE PINECONE

When we look at a diagram of Enlil or Enki, we notice that they are carrying two things. The first is some sort of male handbag with a strap. What is this handbag and what does it contain? It is my belief that this handbag is holding the ME, or a device that acts like a supercomputer or a weapon. In Sumerian stories this ME was coveted by all of the Gods. Whenever one of the Gods slept, (he) was sure to keep it close by his side. But we can also see him holding usually in his right hand something that looks like a Pinecone. Why a pine cone? It is my belief that the pine cone is a symbol of the third eye, or possibly the pineal gland in the brain.

Anunnaki God holding pinecone

Pinecone visible in right hand with bag in left hand.

Eye of Horus compared to human Pineal Gland. See the similarity?

Interesting architecture with Pinecone

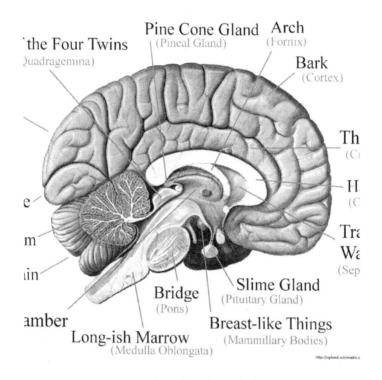

PineCone Gland (Pineal Gland) in Human Brain

Pinecone sculpture at the Vatican

CHAPTER 8

THE CHAINS OF DECEPTION

"The truth is we are not wisely governed by our various global institutions, but rather callously exploited by them"

- Brad Olsen - *Modern Esoteric*

"It is undeniable that religious zealots throughout the ages have routinely destroyed or kept hidden controversial documents that contradicted their own point of view....Much of what we know and believe today about religion is the result of a long tradition of filtering information through the hands of a select few...In fact the book we called the Holy Bible is the product of numerous committees, working under government mandates, dictated by political objectives and is therefore not considered by historians to be a particularly reliable historical document"

- Joe Lewels - *The God Hypothesis*

Rh-negative blood. "Rh" coming from "Rhesus Monkey" factor, meaning our red blood cells have a definate pre-cursor from primates. Rh-negative is very rare. Only 15% of the population has it. But if it didn't arrive through primates, where did it come from?

The Starchild skull - a genuine 900 year old skull found in the 1930's in a cave on Mexico has been proven to be a human-alien hybrid. A DNA test of the skull in 2010 confirms that it is partially of extraterrestrial origin - whose mother was human and father extraterrestrial. The skull demonstrates 10 standard deviations from human skulls in density - the bone is similar to tooth enamel, half as thick and weighing half as much as human bone. However, it is more durable. Just like the "memory metal" found at the Roswell crash, extraterrestrials have created a lighter, more durable form in order to evolve.

These examples further demonstrate the myths being perpetuated in every belief system of humankind, both secular and religious. The purpose of these myths is to distort the truth about our human origins. If it is logical to assume that intelligence increases century by century as human beings develop, then why is it that the ancient Egyptians and

Sumerians were more technically advanced then the later Romans and Europeans? It just doesn't make sense.

The Canadian Anthropologist and author Jeremy Narby says the following about DNA - "*DNA and the cell based life it codes for are an extremely sophisticated technology that far surpasses our present understanding and that was initially developed elsewhere than on Earth.*"

What if I told you that a famous Pulitzer Prize winning author and intellectual wrote a scientific paper in 1962 (six years before von Daniken's book "Chariots of the Gods") that was suppressed by NASA and the Pentagon in 1964? This paper revealed a comprehensive model of Ancient Aliens that adhered to all the rules of the scientific method. It was peer-reviewed and published in the scientific journal, **Planetary and Space Science**, and then something incredible happened. It disappeared. No one spoke about it, no one critiqued it, and no one ever referenced it. The following are some excerpts from this scientific paper-

"*By terrestrial analogy it is not unreasonable to expect that, over astronomical timescales, intelligence and technical civilizations will evolve on many life-bearing planets. Under such circumstances the possibility then looms that contact with other Galactic communities may somehow be established.*"

The purpose of the present paper is to explore the likelihood and possible consequences of another Communications Channel: direct physical contact among Galactic communities by relativistic Interstellar spaceflight.

The statistics presented earlier in this paper suggests that the Earth has been visited by various Galactic Civilizations many times during geological time. It is not out of the question that artifacts of these visits still exist, or even that some kind of base is maintained within the solar system to provide continuity for successive expeditions. Because of weathering and the possibility of detection and interference by the inhabitants of the earth, it would be preferable not to erect such a base on the Earth's surface. The moon seems one reasonable alternative."

The paper was written by Carl Sagan at Stanford University.

Sagan actually coined the term exobiology - *The branch of biology that focuses on the search for extraterrestrial life and the conditions conducive to the development of life, often using the techniques of astronomy to make measurements or observations.*

Author Donald L.Zygutis remarks - *"The Skeptics have created a false choice narrative that states that anything that has to do with ancient alienism is, a priori, pseudo-scientific, and that any individual who advocates ancient alienism is, by inference, a charlatan. Leaders of all three institutions- NASA, SETI, and professional skepticism - have a vested interest in hiding the truth that Carl Sagan, the great alien hunter and skeptic par excellence, never, throughout his entire life, recanted his view that Earth has been visited by aliens."* (page 119).

He continues - *"In a 14 billion year old Universe, aliens even a mere ten million years ahead of us would have the entire galaxy mapped and explored, and every planet that was amenable to life, including ours, visited numerous times. Though it may involve rockets, it's not rocket science."*. (page 145).

Carl Sagan

CHAPTER 9

TRUTH BE TOLD

January 4th 1999 - NASA officially recognized the possibility that life on Earth comes from space

March 19th 1999 - NASA scientists announced that two more meteorites held even stronger fossilized evidence for past life on Mars.

May 11th 2001 - geologist Bruno D'Argenio and molecular biologist Giuseppe Geraci from the University of Naples announced that they had found extraterrestrial bacteria inside a meteorite estimated to be more than 4.5 billion years old.

January 25th 2005 - J. Craig Venter a biologist involved in sequencing the human genome, endorsed panspermia.

May 10th 2007 - eminent biologist E.O. Wilson endorsed panspermia.

April 18th 2008 - Richard Dawkins, and evolutionary biologist, endorsed panspermia.

April 7th 2009 - Stephen Hawking, a world-renowned physicist, endorsed panspermia.

The observable universe is currently believed to have at least 80 billion galaxies. That's 80,000,000,000 galaxies! Imagine even if there are a minimum of 50,000 planets that currently have extraterrestrial life in our own Milky Way galaxy, extrapolated to 80,000,000,000 galaxies. It's unimaginable that we are the only sentient beings in space. It is impossible.

Author Will Hart puts it perfectly - *"When we look at and carefully examine the Great Pyramid, we find the automobile preceding the wheeled cart"*. Hart - page 45

Doesn't this apply to man? The Egyptians were more technically advanced then the medieval Europeans almost 1,000 years later. Sumerians described Uranus, Neptune and Plato in their clay tablets thousands of years before these planets were even discovered by telescope. They described DNA being the "essence of man" thousands of years before DNA was discovered. They told us that man was created by the Anunnaki, as slaves to lighten their burden. Why wouldn't we believe them? Is this the "missing link"?

How did we get from 48 down to 46 chromosomes considering there is a genetic wall preventing such a reproductive a union? This could not have happened through traditional Darwinistic evolution. **It could only have happened through an external manipulation of the human**

genome. The Annunaki added and inserted new genes - 223 of which are perfect examples. Vitamin B12 also known as cobalamin, can be found in several copies only in humans on chromosome 2. Chimpanzees only have one copy. B12 is a direct component of brain development which explains the massive increase from 950cc to 1350cc in only 50,000 years of human development. Isn't it interesting that the cobalamin metabolic pathway is more likely to have evolved on a cobalt -rich planet. What is one example of a cobalt-rich planet, (drum roll please)..........Nibiru!

The truth has now been told.

Man is not a direct descendant of ape - he is a direct descendant of Anunnaki. It can be proven through 223 genes without predecessors and specifically in Chromosome-2. In my thee books - "Adam=Alien", "Adam Decoded" and "Adam–The Missing Link", I have set out to prove this. Through the recent Military video footage of UFO's, there is a "slow leak" by the Elite to prepare us for the truth. For almost 100 years, all evidence of extraterrestrials has been hidden from us because the Elite thought this information would cause "worldwide chaos". It won't.

We all know why it was hidden - **power**. Their efforts to withhold this vital information keeps them in power, keeps their industries humming and making lots of money, and to top it all off, they use religion to enslave us even further. Keeping us numb. They relish in the fact that we watch sitcoms during the week, football on Saturdays and go to places of worship on Sundays. Perfect! No interest in finding out where we are really from, why we haven't used Tesla's wireless energy since 1920, and why we really worship our God.

Power. Money. Slavery.

This is the Elite's trinity.

But no more. There are critical thinkers all over the globe today that are onto their scheme. We know the game. We figured it out, and we will expose it. I encourage all free-thinkers and open-minded critics to get involved. Push the ideology, push the dogma and push the agenda. We all pay enormous amounts of taxes, and yes, we are entitled. We are entitled to know where we are really from. We are entitled to know why innocent scientists, politicians, and free-thinkers are muffled and chastised for espousing their criticisms of "holes" in science, and freedom of speech. There are many holes, as I've outlined in this book, that prove that man is a product of extraterrestrial bio-engineering - not evolution or the big "G". We are all incredible examples of vast intelligence, creativity and innovation. We all have a little "g" in all of us - in our DNA - which is still the greatest mystery of all.

Could our DNA be the answer to the question of man's origins?

Or maybe it's initials actually stand for - "**D**escendant of **N**ibiru and **A**nunnaki"

"I will choose a path that's clear-

I will choose free will."

-Neil Peart – Rush

BIBLIOGRAPHY

1. *"God Games"* - Neil Freer

2. *"Sapiens Rising"* - Neil Freer

3. *"Everything You Know is Wrong"* - Lloyd Pye

4. *"DNA of the Gods"* - Chris H. Hardy, Ph.D

5. *"Anunnaki Theory Authenticated"* - Shafak GokTurk

6. *"The God Code"* - Gregg Braden

7. *"The Cosmic Serpent"* - Jeremy Narby

8. *The God Hypothesis"* - Joe Lewels

9. *"Voices from Legendary Times"* - Ellen Lloyd

10. "The Sagan Conspiracy" - Donald L. Zygutis

11. "Ancient Alien Ancestors" - Will Hart

12. www.earthancients.com - Bruce Fenton

APPENDIX

ARTICLE #1 BY JOHN STOKES

In www.agoracosmopolitan.com,
republished by Exopolitics News from September 12, 2020
Scientists find Extraterrestrial genes in Human DNA
Do civilizations of advanced human beings exist scattered in the Galaxy?
by John Stokes

> Eyewitness testimony of Asket, the extraterrestrial human woman, reference: www.gaiaguys.net

A group of researchers working at the Human Genome Project indicate that they made an astonishing scientific discovery: They believe so-called 97% non-coding sequences in human DNA is no less than genetic code of extraterrestrial life forms.

The non-coding sequences are common to all living organisms on Earth, from moulds to fish to humans. In human DNA, they constitute larger part of the total genome, says Prof. Sam Chang, the group leader. Non-coding sequences, originally known as "junk DNA", were discovered years ago, and their function remained a mystery. The overwhelming majority of Human DNA is "Off-world" in origin. The apparent "extraterrestrial junk genes" merely "enjoy the ride" with hard working active genes, passed from generation to generation.

After comprehensive analysis with the assistance of other scientists, computer programmers, mathematicians, and other learned scholars, Professor Chang had wondered if the apparently "junk Human DNA" was created by some kind of "extraterrestrial programmer".

The alien chunks within Human DNA, Professor Chang further observes, "have its own veins, arteries, and its own immune system that vigorously resists all our anti-cancer drugs."

Professor Chang further stipulates that "Our hypothesis is that a higher extraterrestrial life form was engaged in creating new life and planting it on various planets. Earth is just one of them. Perhaps, after programming, our creators grow us the same way we grow bacteria in Petri dishes. We can't know their motives - whether it was a scientific experiment, or a way of preparing new planets for colonization, or is it long time ongoing business of seedling life in the universe."

Professor Chang further indicates that "If we think about it in our human terms, the apparent "extraterrestrial programmers" were most probably working on "one big code" consisting of several projects, and the projects should have produced various life forms for various planets. They have been also trying various solutions. They wrote "the big code", executed it, did not like some function, changed them or added new one, executed again, made more improvements, tried again and again."

Professor Chang's team of researchers furthermore concludes that, "The apparent "extraterrestrial programmers" may have been ordered to cut all their idealistic plans for the future when they concentrated on the "Earth project" to meet the pressing deadline. Very likely in an apparent rush, the "extraterrestrial programmers" may have cut down drastically on big code and delivered basic program intended for Earth."

Professor Chang is only one of many scientists and other researchers who have discovered extraterrestrial origins to Humanity.

> Human Genome Project Coordinators find absolute proof of
> Extraterrestrial contact with 'Earth humans' via DNA evidence.

Professor Chang and his research colleagues show that apparent "extraterrestrial programming" gaps in DNA sequencing precipitated by a hypothesized rush to create human life on Earth presented humankind with illogical growth of mass of cells we know as cancer."

Professor Chang further indicates that "What we see in our DNA is a program consisting of two versions, a big code and basic code." Mr. Chang then affirms that the "First fact is, the complete 'program' was positively not written on Earth; that is now a verified fact. The second fact is, that genes by themselves are not enough to explain evolution; there must be something more in 'the game'."

"Soon or later", Professor Chang says "we have to come to grips with the unbelievable notion that every life on Earth carries genetic code for his extraterrestrial cousin and that evolution is not what we think it is."

Human Genome Project Discovery Implications associated with "Human-looking Extraterrestrials"

The implications of these scientific finds would reinforce claims by other scientists and observers of having contact with 'off-world' human looking extraterrestrials.

The 'off-world' human looking extraterrestrial have been claimed to have provided some of the genetic material for human evolution, and that many of these extraterrestrials have allowed some of their personnel to incarnate as 'star seeds' on Earth in human families. These "star seeds", "star children" or "star people" are described by Brad and Francie Steiger as individuals whose 'souls' were formally incarnated on the worlds of other star systems and then traveled to Earth and decided to incarnate here in order to "boost" the spiritual evolutionary development of humanity. Most of humanity would consider this group of extraterrestrials to be 'benevolent' as described by 'contactees' such as George Adamski, Orfeo Angelucci, George Van Tassell, Howard Menger, Paul Villa, Billy Meier and Alex Collier who each explain the nature of their voluntary interactions with these human looking extraterrestrials. These "contactees" often provide physical evidence in the form of photographs, film and/or witnesses of their contacts with extraterrestrial races. The most extensively documented and researched contactee is Eduard 'Billy' Meier who provided much physical evidence for investigators.

Representations concerning 'Ancient astronauts'

Indeed, 'ancient astronaut' writers believe that a race of intelligent extraterrestrial beings visited and/or colonised Earth in the remote past, whereupon they upgraded the primitive hominid *Homo erectus* by means of genetic engineering to create the human race as we know it: *Homo sapiens.*

Evidence for this idea is found (a) in the improbability of *Homo sapiens* emerging so suddenly, according to the principles of orthodox Darwinism; and (b) in the myths of ancient civilisations which describe human-like gods coming down from the heavens and creating mankind 'in their own image'.*Homo sapiens* is thus regarded as a hybrid being, incorporating a mix of terrestrial genes from *Homo erectus* and extraterrestrial genes from an ascribed "race of the gods".

Prior to the modern age of space travel and genetics, this theory for the origins of humankind could not have been conceived. And even now, in the 21st century, there are many people who would regard it as science fiction. However, in the light of the problems with the orthodox theory of human evolution, the idea of a genetic intervention by an intelligent human-like species (who themselves evolved on another planet over a more credible time frame) does require to be taken seriously as a potential solution to the mystery.

The most famous exponents of the ancient astronaut intervention are the Swiss writer Erich von Daniken and the American writer Zecharia Sitchin. The latter, in particular, has argued the case in great detail.

Representation by academics from "Exopolitics" groups

Dr. Micheal E. Salla is one of the founders of an Exopolitics movement which seeks an open and informed dialogue on, and with, Extraterrestrials, toward the affirmation of "global democracy" and the quality-of-living of humankind as socially responsible beings in the Universe. Dr. Salla indicates that "There are an extensive number of extraterrestrial races known [by various research institutions and agencies] to be currently interacting with Earth and the human population.

Dr. Salla, is also the author of Exopolitics: Political Implications of the Extraterrestrial Presence (Dandelion Books, 2004). He has held full time academic appointments at the Australian National University, and American University, Washington DC. He has a Ph.D. in Government from the University of Queensland, Australia. During his professional academic career, he was best known for organizing a series of citizen diplomacy initiatives for the East Timor conflict funded by U.S. Institute of Peace and the Ford Foundation. He is also the Founder of the Exopolitics Institute ; and Chief Editor of the *Exopolitics Journal'* and

Convener of the "Extraterrestrial Civilizations and World Peace Conference."

In a 1998 interview, Clifford Stone, a retired U.S. army Sergeant who served in the U.S. Army for 22 years and allegedly participated in operations to retrieve crashed extraterrestrial ships and extraterrestrial biological entities (EBE's), revealed there were a variety of extraterrestrial races known [by various institutions and agencies]". Dr. Salla further elaborates that "The most compelling testimonies on the different extraterrestrial races comes from 'whistleblowers' such as Sergeant Stone; and also 'contactees' who have had direct physical contact with extraterrestrials and communicated with them."

Dr. Salla further notes that Master Sergeant Bob Dean had a twenty seven year distinguished career in very senior areas of the military indicates that among the know extraterrestrials one group "looked so much like us they could sit next to you on a plane or in a restaurant and you'd never know the difference."

Apparently "Human extraterrestrial races can easily integrate with human society in the manner described by Dean and others where they can be indistinguishable from the rest of humanity." Dr. Salla corroborates.

According to Alex Collier who claims to be a "contactee", "a variety of extraterrestrial races have provided genetic material for the 'human experiment'. " Alex Collier indicates that "Earth humans" are "a product of extraterrestrial genetic manipulation, and are possessors of a vast gene pool consisting of many different racial memory banks, also consisting of at least 22 different races."

Alleged Human ET efforts to promote the unity of humanity through religious spirituality

Alex Collier further claims that constituents of "Human ETs" seek to "ensure that global humanity evolves in a responsible way without endangering both itself and the greater galactic community of which it is part. " Exopolitics groups and independent contactees also indicate that constituents of "Human ETs" seek to "uplift human consciousness and to promote the unity of religion."

Alex Colliers alleged contact with ETs suggest that fundamentalist messages in from Christianity to Judaism to Islam, and other institutionalized religions, as well as outright apparent 'cult' groups, have been specifically placed by "hostile elements" to manipulate and control humankind.

Jesus, who many groups allege was a "Human ET" sought to inspire the social consciousness of humankind toward unity, and not to create a "Christian religion", with its sexually repressive as well as homophobic undertones, which also have been used for the execution of racism, and to legitimate atrocities like the 'slave trade'.

ETs who allegedly contacted Alex Collier, also further allegedly stipulate that Jesus did in fact live; and lived out the rest of his life in Massada; and that Jesus was only crucified through the religious doctrine, and myth-making associated with 'the palms'.

As far as the "saviour scenario" is concerned, for example, Alex Collier was allegedly told by ETs that it has been put into our belief systems to "disempower us." The saviour scenario within the dogma of institutionalized religions legitimate the creation of an elite-driven oppressive power structure who appoint themselves as "judgers of morality". These religious elites have historically used their self-appointed roles to execute a comprehensive system of social controls that complement their joint pursuit of greed-oriented self-aggrandizement with other elites from government to business enterprises.

The alleged efforts of socially progressive Human ETs to inspire the affirmation of the quality-of-living of 'Earth Humans' through spiritual and other "emissaries", have been undermined by the efforts of "capitalists" to exploit such alleged initiatives in the pursuit of an oppressive agenda of greed and fascistic power.

Constituents of Human ETs allegedly seek to "help humanity find freedom from oppressive structures through education and consciousness raising."

Allegations of "Human ET" encounters on Earth

In Dr. Salla's article "Extraterrestrials Among Us" published in October 2006, he alleges that, "There is startling evidence from a number of independent sources that 'human looking' extraterrestrial visitors have integrated with and lived in major population centres up until recently, and this is known by a select number of institutions.

Aside from whistleblower testimonies, like Sergeant Major Robert Dean, a number of private individuals claim to have encountered extraterrestrials posing as ordinary citizens in major cities around the planet.

George Adamski was the first to write about extraterrestrials secretly living among the human population. In his second non-fiction book describing his extraterrestrial contact experiences, "Inside the Flying Saucers", Adamski discussed how human looking extraterrestrials had established a presence among the human population. "They apparently looked so much like us", Dr. Salla notes "that they could get jobs, lived in neighbourhoods, drove cars, and could blend in easily with the human population."

Dr. Salla further notes that "Adamski wrote about how they contacted him to set up meetings that led to his famous flights aboard extraterrestrial vehicles." But as Dr. Salla explains "While controversy over Adamski's contact experiences and his credibility continues, Adamski's UFO sightings and contacts with extraterrestrials were supported by an impressive collection of witnesses, photographs and films that a number of independent investigators concluded were not hoaxes."

Dr. Salla additionally stipulates that "Adamski's testimony offers important insights into how extraterrestrials may be living incognito among the human population. After discussing the Adamski case and the strongest evidence supporting it, Dr. Salla in that article further discusses other contactees similarly claiming to have encountered extraterrestrials acting like ordinary citizens. Finally, Dr. Salla in "Extraterrestrials Among Us" examines the official testimony of a number of whistleblowers concerning knowledge that extraterrestrials live among ordinary Earthbound individuals.

Contact Testimonies of 'Extraterrestrials Among Us'

Adamski's famous "Desert Center" meeting with an extraterrestrial emerging from a 'scout ship' on November 20, 1952 was apparently seen by six witnesses who signed affidavits confirming Adamski's version of events in his subsequent book, *The Flying Saucers have Landed* (1953). In fact, four of the witnesses immediately reported what had happened to a nearby newspaper, the *Phoenix Gazette,* that published a story on November 24 featuring photos and sketches. The Desert Center encounter was among those of Adamski's claims regarding extraterrestrial contact that, according to UFO researcher Timothy Good, were "accurately reported," and "sensible and verifiable", as footnotes by Dr. Salla. Given the clear supporting evidence supporting Adamski's first meeting with an extraterrestrial traveling in a scout craft, it is worth examining closely his alleged subsequent meetings with extraterrestrials living on Earth.

In the first chapter of *Inside the Flying Saucers,* Dr. Salla re-visits Adamski's testimony of his meeting with two extraterrestrials while he was sitting in the lobby of a Los Angeles Hotel on February 18, 1953.

"I looked at my wrist watch and saw that it said ten-thirty. The lateness of the hour, with still nothing of extraordinary significance having taken place, sent a wave of disappointment through me. And just at this moment of depression, two men approached, one of whom addressed me by name. Both were complete strangers, but there was no hesitancy in their manner as they came forward, and nothing in their appearance to indicate that they were other than average young businessmen. I noted that both men were well proportioned. One was slightly over six feet and looked to be in his early thirties. His complexion was ruddy, his eyes dark brown, with the kind of sparkle that suggests great enjoyment of life. His gaze was extraordinarily penetrating. His black hair waved and was cut according to our style. He wore a dark brown business suit but no hat. The shorter man looked younger and I judged his height to be about five feet, nine inches. He had a round boyish face, a fair complexion and eyes of grayish blue. His hair, also wavy and worn in our style, was sandy in color. He was dressed in a gray suit and was also hatless. He smiled as he addressed me by name. As I acknowledged the greeting, the speaker extended his hand and when it touched mine a great joy filled me. The signal was the same as had been given by the man I had met on the desert on that memorable November 20, 1952. (Described in the book *Flying Saucers Have Landed*)."

Significant in Adamski's description is how the two extraterrestrials could pass off as businessmen. Aside from a penetrating stare, nothing struck him as unusual in their appearance.

Adamski goes on to explain how he went with them in their car to travel to a remote desert location:

"Together we left the lobby, I walking between them. About a block north of the hotel, they turned into a parking lot where they had a car waiting. They had not spoken during this short time, yet inwardly I knew that these men were true friends. I felt no urge to ask where they proposed to take me, nor did it seem odd that they had volunteered no information. An attendant brought the car around, and the younger man slid into the driver's seat, motioning me to get in beside him. Our other companion also sat with us on the front seat. The car was a four-door black Pontiac sedan. The man who had taken the wheel seemed to know exactly where he was going and drove skillfully. I am not familiar with all the new highways leading out of Los Angeles, so I had no idea in which direction we were headed. We rode in silence and I remained entirely content to wait for my companions to identify themselves and explain the reason for our meeting."

"What's significant here is that the two extraterrestrials possessed a car and knew how to navigate on the newly completed Los Angeles highway system. This is no mean feat and suggests that the extraterrestrials had taken the time to learn the road traffic rules and how to navigate through Los Angeles."

Dr. Salla indicates in "Extraterrestrials Among Us", that Adamski further reveals:

"Lights and dwellings thinned as we left the outskirts of the city. The taller man spoke for the first time. His voice was soft and pleasant and his English perfect. I had noticed that the younger man also spoke softly, although his voice was pitched higher. I found myself wondering how and where they had learned to speak our language so well."

"We are what you on Earth might call 'Contact men.' We live and work here, because, as you know, it is necessary on Earth to earn money with which to buy clothing, food, and the many things that people must have. We have lived on your planet now for several years. At first we did have a slight accent. But that has been overcome and, as you can see, we are unrecognized as other than Earth men. "At our work and in our leisure time we mingle with people here on Earth, never betraying the secret that we are inhabitants of other worlds. That would be dangerous, as you well know. We understand you people better than most of you know yourselves and can plainly see the reasons for many of the unhappy conditions that surround you."

Dr. Salla indicates also that, "This passage [previous] is significant since it describes how the extraterrestrials have spent years living on Earth, learning the language, getting jobs and mixing with the human population. Furthermore, it appears as though extraterrestrials living among the human population may work in pairs, a kind of buddy system that would make sense in terms of ensuring safety and communications with the home world if an emergency ever occurred. If Adamski is accurate in his recollections and the extraterrestrials are telling the truth, then it would appear that there could be a significant number of extraterrestrials who are living incognito among the normal population in many if not most major cities on the planet. Upon examining other contactee cases and the testimonies of whistleblowers, it does appear as though this is indeed the case."

Exopolitics groups furthermore provide additional representation that Adamski was not the only one of the contactees making representation that extraterrestrials were blending in with the human population. Howard Menger, for example. also claimed to have been contacted by extraterrestrials posing as ordinary human citizens. In one case, the extraterrestrial was posing as a real estate salesperson and asked Menger to accompany him in one of the extraterrestrial's vehicle.

In addition to seeking to learn about human values and civilization, it appears that "Human ET" visitors were conducting a low key education effort to promote awareness of their presence to a limited number of individual 'contactees'.

These "Human extraterrestrial visitors" have been represented has often having as very attractive physical characteristics, with "Human extraterrestrial females" being described as among the most beautiful women that male observers have witnessed.

The "Human extraterrestrials visitors" furthermore have been represented as going to great trouble in learning the indigenous language of the culture they are immersed in, learning how to drive and navigate on highways systems, and taking innocuous jobs over several years.

Extraterrestrials living among us appear to be operating in a manner similar to a "celestial peace corps" where they try to blend in. They presumably wish to learn about Earth culture and behaviour; and to, perhaps, assist in passing on information to selected individuals.

Representation on Earth Humans relative to "non-Earthbound" humans:

Advanced Human ETs as viewing Earth Humans as barbarians and savages which are a threat to themselves

Alex Collier alleges that ETs revealed to his that there are over 135 other billion human beings in the 8 galaxies closest to ours.

Alex Collier alleges that "The first time I walked on to one of their ships [Human ETs] , a bunch of their children started to run away from me. They knew that I was from Earth."

"We have a very bad reputation," Alex Collier indicates, "because we are the only human race in the galaxy that kills itself, that turns on itself. We are the only race [human] that allows itself to live in poverty. We are the only ones who allow members of our race to starve. We are the only ones that allow members of the race to be homeless. We are the only race that would sell itself into slavery. I don't like the reflection they give me of us. It's not that they are judging. They just don't understand why we do it. If anyone's got an answer for it, I'm open. Yes, we've been manipulated by belief systems, but why do we believe these belief systems?"

According to testimony by Alex Collier in associated with alleged ET contacts, Earth Humans "are the only race of human beings which oppresses and kills itself."

If Human ETs do exist, as scholarly and other representation suggests, the saving of Humanity from its current apparent course of self-destruction, including on-going catastrophic Global Warming, may very well vitally rely on human governance systems placing its greed-driven bigotries aside, toward a constructive dialogue.

ARTICLE #2 BY CZECH HEALTH MAGAZINE

New findings about "junk DNA" may bring some surprises. _Czech_ (http://www.gewo.applet.cz/health/DNA_1.htm) A group of researchers working at the Human Genome Project will be announcing soon that they made an astonishing scientific discovery: They believe so-called non-coding sequences (97%) in human DNA is no less than genetic code of an unknown extraterrestrial life form.

The non-coding sequences are common to all living organisms on Earth, from molds to fish to humans. In human DNA, they constitute larger part of the total genome, says Prof. Sam Chang, the group leader. Non-coding sequences, also known as "junk DNA", were discovered years ago, and their function remains mystery. Unlike normal genes, which carry the information that intracellular machinery uses to synthesize proteins, enzymes and other chemicals produced by our bodies, non-coding sequences are never used for any purpose. They are never expressed, meaning that the information they carry is never read, no substance is synthesized and they have no function at all. We exist on only 3% of our DNA. The junk genes merely enjoy the ride with hard working active genes, passed from generation to generation. What are they? How come these idle genes are in our genome? Those were the question many scientists posed and failed to answer - until the breakthrough discovery by Prof. Sam Chang and his group.

Trying to understand the origins and meaning of junk DNA Prof. Chang realized that he first needs a definition of "junk". Is junk DNA really junk, (useless and meaningless) or it contains some information not claimed by the rest of DNA for whatever reason? He once mentioned the question to an acquaintance, Dr. Lipshutz, a young theoretical physicist turned Wall Street derivative securities specialist. "Easy," replied Lipshutz. "We'll run your sequence through the software I use to analyze market data, and it will show if your sequences are total garbage, "white noise", or there is a message in there." This new breed of analysts with strong background in math, physics and statistics are getting more and more popular with Wall Street firms. They sift through gigabytes of market statistics, trying to uncover useful correlation between the various market indexes, and individual stocks.

Working evenings and weekends, Lipshutz managed to show that non-coding sequences are not all junk, they carry information. Combining massive database of the Human Genome Project with thousands of data files developed by geneticists all over the world Lipshutz calculated Kolmogorov entropy of the non-coding sequences and compared it with the entropy of regular, active genes.

Kolmogorov entropy, introduced by the famous Russian mathematician half a century ago, was successfully used to quantify the level of randomness in various sequences, from time sequences of noise in radio lamps to sequences of letters in 19th century Russian poetry. By and large, the technique allows researchers to quantitatively compare various sequences and conclude which one carries more information than the other does. "To my surprise, the entropy of coding and non-coding DNA sequences was not that different", continues Lipshutz.

"There was noise in both but it was no junk at all. If the market data were that orderly, I would have already retired." After a year of cooperation with Lipshutz, Chang was convinced, there is a hidden information in junk DNA. However, how could one understand its meaning if the information is never used? With active sequences you try to watch the cell and see what proteins are being made using the information. This wouldn't work with dormant genes. There will be experiment to test a hypothesis; one should rely on the power of his thought. Since there are letters, it should be tested in some old languages, perhaps Sumerian, Egyptian, Hebrew, and so on. Prof. Sam Chang solicited help from three specialists in the field, but none of them managed to find a solution. There were no cultural clues, no references to other known languages, the field was too alien for the linguists.

"I asked myself: who else can decipher a hidden message?" Chang continues.

"Of course, cryptographers! In addition, I began talking with researchers at the National Security Agency. It took me few months to make them return my calls. Were they running background checks on me? Alternatively, were they too busy lobbying senators on retaining and strengthening their authority to control exports of encryption technologies? Eventually, a junior fellow was assigned to answer my questions. He listened, requested my questions in writing and after another, few months turned me down. His message was polite but meant, "Go to hell with your crazy ideas. We are a serious agency, its National Security, dude. We are too busy."

Well, Sam, forget the Government, talk to the private sector. Therefore, I began approaching computer security consultants. They were genuinely interested, and a couple of them even began working on my project, but their enthusiasm always faded after a month. I kept calling them until one nice fellow told me: "I'd love to work on your project if I had more time. I am overbooked. Emissaries of major banks and Fortune 500 companies are begging me to plumb the holes in their networks. They pay me $500

an hour. I can give you an educational discount, can you afford $350?"
Scrambling $15/hr for a post doctoral studies is a big deal in academia,
$350 sounded as something extraorbital."

Eventually Prof. Chang was referred to Dr. Adnan Mussaelian, a talented
cryptographer in the former Soviet republic of Armenia. Poor fellow
barely survived on a $15 a month salary and occasional fees for tutoring
children of Armenian nuveau riches. A $10,000 research grant was a
struck of luck, he began working like a beaver.

Adnan promptly confirmed the findings of his Wall Street predecessor:
The entropy indicated tons of information almost in the clear, it was not
too strong cryptographic system, it didn't appear to be a tough problem.
Adnan began applying differential cryptoanalysis and similar standard
cryptographic techniques.

He was two months in the project when he noticed that all non- coding
sequences are usually preceded by one short DNA sequence. A very
similar sequence usually followed the junk. These segments, known to
biologists as alu sequences, were all over the whole human genome. Being
non-coding, junk sequences themselves, alu are one of the most common
genes of all. Trained as a cryptographer and computer programmer, and
having no knowledge of microbiology, Adnan approached the genetic
code as of computer code. Dealing with 0, 1, 2, 3 (four bases of genetic
code) instead of 0s and 1s of the binary code was a sort of nuisance, but
the computer code was what he was analyzing and deciphering all his life.
He was on familiar territory. The most common symbol in the code that
causes no action followed by a chunk of dormant code. What is that? Just
playing with the analogy Adnan grabbed the source code of one his
programs and fed it into the program that calculates the statistics of
symbols and short sequences, a tool often used in decoding messages.

What was the most common symbol? Of course, it was "/", a symbol of comment! He took a Pascal code, and it were { and } ! Of course, the code between two slashes in C is never executed, and is never meant to be executed; it is not the code, it is the comment to the code!

Being unable to resist the temptation to further play with the analogy, Adnan began comparing statistical distributions of the comments in computer and genetic code. There must be a striking difference. This should show up in statistics. Nevertheless, statistically, junk DNA was not much different from active, coding sequences. To be sure, Adnan fed a program into the analyzer: surprisingly, the statistics of code and comments were almost the same. He looked into the source code and realized why: there were very few comments in between the slashes, it was mostly C code the author decided to exclude from execution, a common practice among programmers. Adnan, religiously inclined person, was thinking about the divine hand - but after analyzing the spaghetti code inside the sequences he convinced himself that whoever wrote the small code was not God. Who wrote the active, small coding part of human genetic code was not very well organized, he was a rather sloppy programmer. It looked like rather somebody from Microsoft, but at the time human genetic code was written, there was no Microsoft on Earth.

On Earth? It was like a lightning... Was the genetic code for all life on Earth written by an extraterrestrial programmer and then somehow deposited here, for execution? The idea was mad and frightening, and Adnan resisted it for days. Then he decided to proceed. If the non-coding sequences are parts of the program that were rejected or abandoned by the author, there is a way to make them work. The only thing one needs to do is to remove the symbols of comments and if the portion between the /*......*/ symbols is a meaningful routine it may compile and execute!

Following this line of thought, Adnan selected only those non-coding sequences that had exactly the same frequency distribution of symbols as the active genes. This procedure excluded the comments in Marcian or Q, whatever it was. He selected some 200 non-coding sequences that most closely resembled real genes, stripped them of /*, //, and similar stuff and after few days of hesitation sent e-mail to his American boss, asking him to find a way to put them in E-coli or whatever host and make them work. Chang did not replied for two weeks. "I thought I was fired", confessed Dr. Mussaelian. "With every day of his silence I more and more realized how crazy my idea was. Chang would conclude I was a schizophrenic and would terminate the contract. Chang finally responded and, to my surprise, he did not fire me. He had not bought my extraterrestrial theory but agreed to try to make my sequences work."

Biologists have attempted for years to make junk sequences express, without much success. Sometimes nothing turned out; sometimes it was junk again. It was not surprising. Grab an arbitrary portion of the excluded computer code and try to compile it. Most likely, it will fail. At best, it will produce bizarre results. Analyze the code carefully, fish out a whole function from the comments, and you may make it work. Because of careful Mussaelian's statistical analysis 4 of the 200 sequences he selected, began working, producing tiny amounts of a chemical compounds.

"I was anxiously awaiting the response from Chang," says Dr. Mussaelian. "Would it be a more or less normal protein or something out of ordinary? The answer was shocking: it was a substance, known to be produced by several types of leukemia in men and animals. Surprisingly, three other sequences also produced cancer-related chemicals. It no longer looked like a coincidence. When one awakens a viable dormant gene, it produces cancer-related proteins. Researchers began searching Human Genome Project databases for the four genes they isolated from junk DNA. Eventually, three of the four were found there, listed as active, non-junk genes. This was not a big surprise: since cancer tissues produce the protein, there must be somewhere a gene, which codes it! The surprise came later: In the active, non-junk portion of the code the gene in question (the researchers called it "jhlg1", for junk human leukemia gene) was not preceded by the alu sequence, i.e. the /* symbol was missing. However, the closing */ symbol at the end of "jhlg1" was there. This explained why "jhlg1" was not expressed in the depth of the junk DNA but worked fine in the normal, active part of the genome. The one who wrote the basic genetic code for humans excluded portion of the big code by embracing them in /*... */ but missed some of the opening /* symbol. His compiler seems to be garbage, too: a good compiler, even from terrestrial Microsoft, would most likely refuse to compile such program at all. Prof. Sam Chang with his students began searching for genes associated with various cancers, and almost in all instances they discovered that those genes are followed by the alu sequence (i.e. protein as a comment closing symbol */), but never preceded by the comment opening /* gene! "This explains why diseases result in cell damage and their death, whereas cancers lead to cell reproduction and growth. Because only few fragments from the big code are expressed, they never lead to coherent growth. What we get with cancer, is expression of only few of genes alien to humans and symbiosis with some genes of bacterial parasites that lead to illogical, bizarre and apparently meaningless chunks of living cells. The chunks have its own veins, arteries, and its own immune system that vigorously resists all our anti-cancer drugs. "Our hypothesis is that a higher extraterrestrial life form was engaged in creating new life and planting it on various planets. Earth is just one of them. Perhaps, after programming, our creators grow us the same way we grow bacteria in Petri dishes. We can't know their motives - whether it was a scientific experiment, or a way of preparing new planets for colonization, or is it long time ongoing business of seedling life in the universe. If we think about it in our human terms, the extraterrestrial programmers were most probably working on one big code consisting of several projects, and the projects should have produced various life forms for various planets. They have been also trying various solutions. They wrote the big code, executed it, did not like some function, changed them or added new one, executed again, made more improvements, tried again and again. Of course, soon or later it was behind schedule. Few deadlines have already passed. Then the management began pressing for an immediate release. The programmers were ordered to cut all their idealistic plans for the future and concentrate now on one (Earth) project to meet the pressing deadline. Very likely in a rush, the programmers cut down drastically the big code and delivered basic program intended for Earth. However, at that time they were (perhaps) not quite certain which functions of the big code may be needed later and which not, so they kept them all there. Instead of cleaning the basic program by deleting all the lines of the big code, they converted them into comments, and in the rush they missed few /* symbols in the comments here or there; thus presenting mankind with illogical growth of mass of cells we know as cancer." There are three options to the problem. Either delete all the /* symbols and comments and clean this way the basic code, or add all the missing */ and avoid illogical mixing of the basic code with the big code. Alternatively, in the third option, remove all the / symbols and let work the basic code with the big code as a complete program. Unfortunately, none of these options are within our capacity. If we were able to efficiently insert genes into the chromosomes of living men, our breakthrough discovery would mean instant cure for all future cancer cases; at least from the programmer point of view. Theoretically, we can do it in a laboratory, but we have no practical means to implant the repaired DNA into living subjects. The mystery of "junk DNA" and cancer seems to be solved, but no quick cure shall be expected. The best thing we can do now is to try nourishing new, cancer-free line of humans with gradually debugged basic genetic code. That will take a long time. For us and our children, there is no hope on the horizon.

"However, from the programmer's point of view, there is also positive outlook in it. What we see in our DNA is a program consisting of two versions, a big code and basic code. First fact is, the complete program was positively not written on Earth; that is now a verified fact. The second fact is, that genes by themselves are not enough to explain evolution; there must be something more in the game. What it is or where it is, we don't kow. The third fact is, no creator of a new work, be it a composer, engineer or programmer, from Mars or Microsoft, will ever leave his work without the option for improvement or upgrade. Ingenious here is, that the upgrade is already enclosed - the "junk DNA" is nothing more than hidden and dormant upgrade of our basic code! We know for some time that certain cosmic rays have power to modify DNA. With this in mind, plausible solution is available. The extraterrestrial programmers may use just one flash of the right energy from somewhere in the Universe to instruct the basic code to remove all the /*...*/ symbols, fuse itself with the big code ("junk DNA") and jumpstart working of our whole DNA. That would change us forever, some of us within months, some of us within generations. The change would be not too much physical, (except no more cancers, diseases and short life), but it will catapult us intellectually. Suddenly, we will be in time comparable to coexistence of Neanderthals with Cro-Magnons.

The old will be replaced giving birth to a new cycle. The complete program is elegant, very clever self-organizing, auto-executing, auto-developing and auto-correcting software for a highly advanced biological computer with build-in connection to the ageless energy and wisdom of the Universe. Software wise, within us is either short and diseased life, or potential for a super- intelligent super-being with a long and healthy life. This triggers puzzling questions - was the reduction to the basic code done by sloppy programmers in a rush (as it appears to us), or was the disabling of the big code purposeful act which can be cancelled by a "remote control" whenever desired?" Soon or later, we have to come to grips with the unbelievable notion that every life on Earth carries genetic code for his extraterrestrial cousin and that evolution is not what we think it is. This discovery may well shake the very roots of humanity - our beliefs in our concept of God and in our own power over our destiny. With the right paradigm, we may discover one day that all forms of life and the whole Universe is just one huge intellectual exercise in thoughts expressed mathematically, by Design, by Creator.

Made in the USA
Middletown, DE
21 May 2021